GIRAFFES

GIRAFFES

Louise C. Brown

Illustrated with photographs by Audrey Ross

DODD, MEAD & COMPANY
New York

ACKNOWLEDGMENTS

The author wishes to express her appreciation to the staff of the San Francisco Zoological Society for their cooperation and assistance in the preparation of this book.

PHOTOGRAPH CREDITS

Norman Myers, Nairobi, pages 41 and 43; San Francisco Zoological Society, pages 33 and 35. All other photographs by Audrey Ross © 1978.

Map on page 14 by Nina Inez Brown.

1 2 3 4 5 6 7 8 9 10

Library of Congress Cataloging in Publication Data

Brown, Louise C
Giraffes.

SUMMARY: Introduces the physical characteristics,
habits, and behavior of giraffes.
1. Giraffes—Juvenile literature. [1. Giraffes]
I. Title.
QL737.U56B76   599'.7357   79-52037
ISBN 0-396-07730-7

*To Rosanne for her invaluable
criticism and assistance*

The giraffe is one of the most amazing animals you are ever likely to see in this world.

Look at it. Have you ever seen anything so tall? Have you ever seen an animal with such long, long legs? Or one with such an incredible, unbelievable neck?

The giraffe is the tallest living creature on the earth.

A full-grown male can measure up to eighteen feet from the bottoms of its hoofs to the tips of its horns. That is three times as tall as a man and more than twice as high as the ceiling in an average room. A female giraffe is only slightly smaller. Even the baby giraffe is almost six feet tall when it is born.

Opposite: *Giraffes are the tallest living creatures on earth.*

But the most astonishing thing about the giraffe is the way it looks. Isn't it all out of proportion? Those legs look like stilts. They are too long and too thin. The head is too small. The ears don't seem the right size. The tail is too stringy. And that tower of a neck! How can a giraffe see where it's going if its head is so far off the ground?

It is puzzling.

Did something go wrong during the evolutionary process? Or did nature have a good reason for giving the giraffe such an odd shape?

For thousands of years people have wondered about this. Some of the natives in Africa thought they knew why and passed the story down so often from one generation to another that it soon became a legend. According to this legend, the giraffe was one of God's experiments. When God had finished creating the world and all the animals in it, the Africans said, He decided to add just one more beast. So He looked around and found some leftover parts of the camel and the antelope and the leopard He had just made. God stuck these spare parts all together, stretched

The "hump" on a giraffe's upper back is really extra large bones and muscles that help support its heavy neck.

the legs and neck of His new creation to make it different, and then sat back to see if the new animal would work out.

It is not hard to understand why people once thought this was the reason the giraffe happened to be on earth.

Look at the giraffe a little more closely. Aren't there parts of it that really do look like a camel? It has the same knobby knees, the same droopy nose, the same solid squat body. It even has a small hump on the back of its shoulders. On the other hand, there is something about the giraffe that reminds one of an antelope, or a deer. Is it because of that gentle, endearing expression on its face and those delicate thin legs? But why would an animal that large need to have spots? It couldn't be for camouflage. A giraffe is surely too big to hide.

It is no wonder that people down through history have always scratched their heads in amazement when they first saw a giraffe.

The pharaohs in Egypt used to keep giraffes on the palace grounds to impress royal visitors. The emperors of Rome prized them for their entertainment value at the popular spectacles in the Colosseum where the giraffe was advertised as a *camel-leopard*.

For many people, the giraffe was just an oddity in the world of nature. Few realized that those very features that make the giraffe look so odd—the exaggerated legs and neck—are the very features that have helped it survive for millions of years.

Take those long legs, for instance.

Did you know that the giraffe can outrun its enemies and race at speeds up to thirty-five miles an hour? Few other animals can do this.

Galloping across a road in Meru National Park. Giraffes can race along at thirty-five miles an hour.

And did you know that those long legs can be powerful, deadly weapons? For all their fragile appearance, those legs are strong enough to crush a lion's skull with one savage kick. In a fight between a giraffe and a lion, it is usually the giraffe that's the winner.

Then there is that extraordinary, elongated neck.

Did you know that the giraffe's neck, more than anything else, has helped the giraffe stay alive? Because its neck is so very long, the giraffe can find food in treetops and

A giraffe can find food in places no other animal can reach.

Keen eyesight and hearing protect it against predators. A giraffe can see as far away as a mile and can distinguish colors.

places that no other animal can reach. It doesn't have to compete with other animals to find enough to eat. And because of its long neck, it has a built-in observation post to keep an eye out for predators. With its keen eyesight and special lookout tower, the giraffe can see as far away as a mile. It can look right over shrubs and into ravines where lions might be hiding. If an enemy is approaching, the giraffe will know it.

13

Giraffes come from Africa. This is the only place where they are found in the wild. Some live in the bush and grassland of East Africa. Others seem to like the tree-dotted plains of the *savanna* in the central part of the continent. And some make their home farther south in the dry *bushveld*, or thornbush country, that stretches from Angola to Rhodesia.

That is where you can see them wandering over the open range along with waterbucks and zebras, with impalas, wildebeests, and ostriches. They walk slowly and sedately across the grassland.

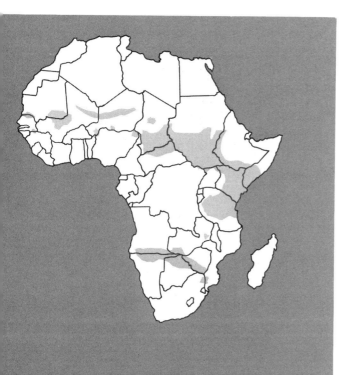

The shaded areas indicate where giraffes are found in Africa.

Above: *A herd of gazelles*. Below: *A herd of zebras*.

A giraffe doesn't simply walk. It strolls. It takes giant steps covering fifteen feet at a stride. A giraffe can move so quietly through the brush, you wouldn't know it was there until you suddenly saw one only a couple of hundred yards away. There it would be standing, still as a statue, just staring down at you.

When a giraffe wants to, it can shift into high gear at a moment's notice. Then it gallops. Tucking its mop of a stringy tail over its back so the tail hair doesn't snag on a thorny bush, a giraffe can clock thirty-five miles an hour in a short burst of speed. And then it is one of the most graceful animals on earth. People who live in Africa say a galloping giraffe looks like a huge rocking horse that seems to float through the air in great leaps and bounds. It seems to sway back and forth across the horizon.

This is undoubtedly why the Arabs call the giraffe *zirafah*. That is an Arabic word that means "creature of grace." It is probably where our English word, giraffe, comes from.

Scientists use both this word and the Roman name, camel-leopard, to form the giraffe's scientific name, *Giraffa camelopardalis*. This name is used only for the giraffe.

At noon, when most animals stay in the shade or mud to keep cool, the giraffe doesn't seem to mind the hot blazing sun. Its large expanse of body surface helps it keep cool.

Giraffes are mammals. They are warm-blooded animals that have backbones. They have lungs to breathe air. And they nurse their young.

Like all other mammals, they have only seven bones, or *vertebrae*, in their necks. Isn't it strange to think that a giraffe would have the same number of bones in its neck as a man or a mouse?

A giraffe's long neck does present some problems that

other mammals don't have. Because it is a warm-blooded animal, it needs to have blood circulating all through its body at a constant pressure. With a giraffe, this means the circulation is mostly up and down. Nature solved this problem by giving the giraffe an extra-large, twenty-five-pound heart so that the blood can be pumped all the way up to its brain. The giraffe also has a special network of tiny valves for the veins and arteries so that it doesn't get dizzy or faint when it suddenly lowers its head to the ground.

This long neck also means that the giraffe has an extraordinarily long windpipe. The giraffe is not mute, as many people believe. It just doesn't use its voice very often. That's because the voice box is so far below its head. It takes a long time for the air to travel all the way up that long windpipe from the chest to the mouth. Sometimes a sharp snort is used to sound a quick alarm to the others in the herd when there is danger.

Opposite: *A giraffe can lift its head up like this because of a special rounded socket at the top of its spinal column.*

A giraffe really doesn't need a voice. Giraffes usually communicate with body language. A flick of an ear or tail, the way the head or neck is held, the manner of walking—all these are ways to "talk" to other giraffes.

For the most part, giraffes are very much alike whether they live in Kenya or the savanna or the bushveld. But there are minor differences in coloring. These differences mean that certain kinds of giraffes belong to different subspecies. There are nine different subspecies, depending on the shape and color of the giraffe's spots. Some giraffes have spots that look "jagged." Some have "leafy" spots. Some have spots that appear to be "blotched." Colors can range from a deep reddish brown to a tawny, light buff or even ivory.

Probably the most handsome of these subspecies is the *reticulated giraffe*. It is usually found in Kenya, Somalia, and parts of Ethiopia. There are narrow, neat, white lines between the big patches of color on this subspecies. So, the reticulated giraffe looks dark in comparison to other giraffes.

The most amazing thing, however, is that there are no

This is a reticulated giraffe, perhaps the most handsome of all the nine subspecies of the Giraffa camelopardalis.

These two giraffes belong to the subspecies called Masai giraffe. Found in parts of Kenya, they have a jagged pattern of spots.

two giraffes in the world with the exact same markings. Even though a giraffe can be identified as belonging to a certain subspecies because of the general shape and coloring of its spots, each giraffe within a subspecies has its own individual color pattern. Just as there are no two people in the world with the exact same fingerprints, there are no two giraffes that have identical spot patterns.

It is not easy to see giraffes in the brush. Despite their size, their spots hide them surprisingly well. If you had a chance to be out there on the savanna during a hot afternoon when all the trees and bushes and landscape seem to shimmer with heat waves, you would have a hard time seeing all the giraffes out there. Some might be "hiding" in between the trees and you wouldn't notice them. It is strange how their spots can be mistaken for shadows of branches against the bark of a tree. Sometimes their necks look just like tree trunks.

Sometimes it's hard to see giraffes when they stand next to dead tree trunks. How many can you count?

This giraffe bends way down to sniff a low bush to find out whether the leaves are fleshy and watery enough to eat.

Giraffes are cud-chewers. They are ruminants like cows and sheep and oxen.

Have you ever watched a cow chew her cud? Do you know how complicated her digestive system is? Giraffes have the same system. First of all, a giraffe has a stomach with four compartments. After a giraffe takes a mouthful of food, it goes down the throat and into stomach compartment number one. There, the food is mashed into little balls. These balls of food are then sent back up to the giraffe's mouth for chewing again. Then the food goes down that long throat again and goes on to compartments two and three and four. So, by the time food reaches the last of the four stomach compartments, you can be sure it is well digested.

What kind of food? Mostly plants, like leaves and thorns and twigs and even bark. Strangely enough, a giraffe does not like grass. What it does like, more than anything else, is the whistling-thorn acacia tree.

Twigs are a tasty item in the daily diet.

The branches of the acacia tree are very thorny. Can you believe that any animal could chew those thorns without cutting its mouth?

The giraffe has no problem. It has long tough hairs on its lips to protect it from those sharp thorns. And its tongue is especially made for this kind of meal. It is as rough as the roughest sandpaper you've ever touched. It is as narrow as a leather strap and is eighteen inches long. A giraffe will curl its tongue around a branch to get a better grip on it. And then, with a quick jerk of its head, the giraffe can wipe the branch clean. Leaves, thorns, and all come off in one swoop.

The giraffe doesn't seem to mind chewing those thorns once they are in its mouth. That's because its tongue is coated with such a thick covering of rubbery saliva, the sharp spikes can't hurt.

A favorite food. Even though colonies of ants live in the round galls you see on this branch of the whistling-thorn acacia, a giraffe will eat the whole thing—ants, galls, thorns, leaves, and all.

This tongue may look long, but it can stretch out twice as far if need be. Eighteen inches in length and rough as sandpaper, a giraffe's tongue is a marvelous grabbing tool.

Salt is a special treat. This giraffe at San Francisco's oceanside zoo has discovered that the fog rolling in from the Pacific almost every day has left a deposit of salt on the fence posts of his pen.

It is estimated that a full-grown giraffe eats about seventy-five pounds of plants each day. Some of this food contains highly nutritious proteins. But three-quarters of this diet is really just water. It is the water that the plants have absorbed from the ground.

Because a giraffe gets most of its needed liquids from plants, it can go for weeks—sometimes even months—without drinking. It doesn't have to depend on rivers and lakes and streams and watering holes for its water supply the way other animals do. During the dry season, when most of the other animals on the savanna are forced to travel long distances in search of water, the giraffe can go where it pleases. It can stay where it is or wander off.

Fortunately for the giraffe, there is no reason to stay near rivers or streams. It doesn't like water. It cannot swim. It will refuse to wade across a shallow creek even though the water is only ankle deep and there are tempting acacia trees on the other side. The giraffe doesn't even like rain. Some naturalists say they've seen a giraffe rush for shelter under the nearest tree at the first sign of rain and then push its head up between the leafy branches so that its face stays dry.

Although a giraffe is free to go where it wishes, it usually keeps within a range of forty to fifty square miles. This is its *home range*.

For the most part, a giraffe doesn't like to huddle to-

gether with lots of other giraffes in large herds the way
other animals do for protection. A herd of giraffes is likely
to be small, rarely more than ten or twelve in a group.
Females prefer to be out in the wide open grassy places
where it is easier to defend their young ones from lions.
Males, on the other hand, would rather be near the edge

*Herds tend to be very small in size, rarely more than ten in one
group.*

With all the room in the world, these two huddle together. Bodily contact seems important—they often rub necks, lick each other's faces, even nose one another's eyes, horns, and manes.

of a thick wooded area where they band together in casual herds. These herds—if you could call these spur-of-the-moment gatherings herds—seem to change from day to day because bulls are rather independent and don't like to stay in the same group too long. Sometimes a bull will leave the area entirely and go off by himself. It usually means that he is ready to mate and will walk alone for miles until he finds a group of females.

Once he has found a mate, he will stay until he is sure she's pregnant. Then it will be fourteen months before her calf is born.

The birth of a giraffe is never an easy time for the mother or her calf. It is a time when lions are likely to attack. The pregnant giraffe knows this only too well. A few days before her baby is due, she searches for just the right kind of hiding place in the brush. It has to be a spot where there is a lot of soft grass on the ground.

When her time comes, she will leave the herd and go off by herself to this place that she has already picked out. If a number of lions are known to be prowling in the area, the rest of the herd will accompany her to this spot and stand in a circle to shield her from danger.

A female giraffe gives birth standing up. This means the newborn calf comes into the world with a jolting drop. The baby is a wet, shaggy little bundle of spindly legs and scrawny neck. Is it possible that within an hour or so he

Opposite: *Just two hours old! This newborn calf at San Francisco Zoo is being encouraged by its mother to stand up. Within an hour after this photograph was taken, the baby was on its feet.*

will manage to get all untangled and stand up by himself? Somehow, he knows how. Waving his neck back and forth, he tries to push his feet and knees into the right position. Up goes his rump. Then he swings his neck back to get his front feet up. Oops! He swings too hard and falls down. He tries again. This time he swings his neck too far forward and falls flat on his face. Another try. And another.

Mooing softly in encouragement, his mother licks his nose and ears and face with her rough tongue. Again he tries to get up. Success! All four wobbly legs are on the ground. He's six feet tall—just the right height to nuzzle under his mother's belly for his first taste of warm milk.

During his first few weeks, a baby giraffe will nurse as often as eight times a day and grow more than an inch every twenty-four hours. By the time he is three weeks old, he is ready to add leaves to his diet and learn how to chew his cud. In a few more months, he will be able to live just on plants, if he has to. But if his mother is nearby, he will continue to nurse for almost a year.

Until very recently, scientists believed that giraffes had little interest in their offspring once the calves were born.

Sometimes there isn't enough milk for the baby and zookeepers must feed the baby with a bottle.

What these observers noticed was that new mothers could be seen wandering off into the brush without their babies. It is now known that giraffes have their own baby-sitting system. During the day, all the calves in a herd are left under the care of one of the females—the "auntie" of the herd. She is the one in charge of the nursery until the mothers return at night.

There is nothing quite as charming as a baby giraffe. He is as frisky and as curious and as inquisitive as a puppy. More often than not, he is likely to spend much of the day scampering behind or between bushes in hopes of getting a closer look at some new, exciting creature he has never seen before. Chameleons, tickbirds, snakes, warthogs, pint-sized dik-diks, marabou storks—anything that moves has to be closely examined. The closer the better. Once in a while he gets too close and is nipped on the nose. Then, with a loud bawl, he runs back to his "auntie" and squeezes underneath her long legs where he knows he will be safe.

By the time a giraffe is one year old, he will be nine feet tall. When he is three, he is just about grown up and anxious to mate. That's when he will begin fighting with other males to see which is stronger.

What a sight it is to see two bulls fighting. It is more of a show of strength than a real fight. Bulls have no intention of seriously hurting each other. But they are serious about winning.

This young calf, a family pet, is looking in a window to see what's going on inside the house. It had been caught in a fence near Lake Naivasha in Africa and then rescued by nearby residents.

While his parents continue eating, this inquisitive young calf can't resist turning around to stare at the photographer.

Head-slamming, some people call it. The object of the match is to land a direct hit with neck, head, horns, or all three at once.

First the challenger walks up to his opponent with a strange stiff-legged step. This means he is ready to fight. Then the two bulls stand shoulder to shoulder, hind legs rigid and far apart. Leaning hard against each other, they push with all their might in hopes of getting the other off balance.

Now the necks go into action. The challenger lowers his head, curves his neck far out like a baseball bat and WHAAM! Neck slams into neck. Then it is the other one's turn. Swinging his neck out on the opposite side and holding his head a bit lower, he twists it so his horns are aimed for a wicked blow. Up comes the neck right underneath the head of the challenger. Up and under and around. The head and horns smack into the challenger's right flank so hard that they're both knocked sideways a few feet. Then it is back into fighting position for both of them. CRAACK! Another solid hit. The sound can be heard a hundred yards away.

A giraffe's horns are hard as ivory and covered with skin. Unlike deer antlers, they are not shed periodically. A female has hairy tufts at the tips of her horns; a male does not. The male has heavier horns, which he uses in fighting.

Shove. Push. Swing. Slam. Clouds of dust are stirred up as the two bulls circle each other like boxers and line up for the big swing.

Finally, after ten or fifteen minutes, the fight is over. One has had enough. Stretching his neck and lifting his nose high up in the air to signal defeat, he turns away. Not content with victory, the winner chases the loser for a short distance and raises his head proudly in triumph.

A bull that has proven he is boss is then free to leave his group, or herd, in search of a female.

There doesn't seem to be any special mating season for giraffes. A cow can become pregnant at any time of the year. During her lifetime of twenty to twenty-five years, she can expect to have at least six calves.

Unfortunately, only one out of three of these baby giraffes will survive beyond their first twelve months.

The lion is the greatest natural threat to the giraffe. It succeeds in killing many calves each year. The most vulnerable time, of course, is when the calf is just born. Another dangerous time in the life of a young giraffe is a few months later when it begins to explore the world around it and wander away from the herd.

But did you know that a lion will rarely attack a full-grown giraffe? A lion must be very, very hungry before he dares to do this. Even then, the lion will think twice. The reason is that the throat of a full-grown giraffe is just too high to reach in one jump. Another reason is that the lion knows the giraffe has a vicious kick. Those long legs are powerfully strong. Those hoofs are hard as stone. One well-aimed kick and the lion is finished.

One of the few times a lion can expect to pull down an adult giraffe is at a water hole. Its neck is long, but not long enough for its mouth to reach the water. The giraffe has to spread its legs far apart when it drinks. It is an awkward position. And it is one of the few times that a lion could grab a giraffe by the throat.

Drinking from the ground can be awkward. The giraffe's legs are just too long. It can either spread its front legs far apart or kneel down. In either case, it's a dangerous position.

The giraffe knows this. When the giraffe comes to a water hole, it looks carefully around to be sure there isn't a lion lurking in the bushes. It first bobs its head up and down a few times before dropping it all the way to the ground. A few sips of water and the giraffe's head pops up again to be sure there is no danger. Then down again to drink some more. And more. If the giraffe has a companion from the herd to stand guard, it will sometimes drink as much as ten gallons at once. That means it can stay away from the dangerous water holes for a long, long time.

Once in a great while lions do succeed in killing a full-grown giraffe, but only if they work as a team. It is not easy. Lying in wait at a safe distance from a herd of male giraffes, the lions keep an eye out for a solitary bull that has just left the herd and is walking alone toward a female herd. Then one or two lions will boldly approach the giraffe from the front while a third lion in the pride creeps up toward the bull from behind. Closer and closer and closer it creeps. Suddenly, with a wild leap and a roar, the lion jumps onto the giraffe's back and sinks its claws and fangs into the animal's back leg. It only takes a few seconds to rip one of those big leg muscles and then the giraffe won't be able to run. But if the lion isn't quick enough, the giraffe heads straight for the nearest thornbush. In no time, the thorns and thick branches are all that are needed to wipe the lion off his back.

Lions would much rather attack baby giraffes. They are easier to kill.

A rare sight. Lions seldom succeed in killing giraffes. When they do, it's usually the females of the pride that do the hunting. This giraffe may have been weakened by illness, which would make it an easy prey for predators.

Giraffes can be affectionate.

If the lion were the only enemy of the giraffe, there wouldn't be any concern about the survival of this remarkable member of the animal kingdom. Unfortunately, there is a much more dangerous enemy. Man. In the past century man has slaughtered countless giraffes.

Native tribesmen have always prized the giraffe. The meat is tasty. The thick hide can be used for water buckets, shields, sandals, and drumheads. The mop-haired tails are used for fly whisks or magic charm bracelets. Recently, however, the slaughter of giraffes has increased at an alarming rate. And it is just to satisfy the thousands of tourists who visit Africa each year and expect to go home with at least one curio made from the skin or bones or hair of a wild animal. Hair bracelets made from the tails of giraffes seem to be especially popular and command such high prices that hunters have been known to kill a giraffe just for its tail.

It would be a tragedy if man succeeded in destroying these gentle giants of the land. The world would never be the same again if they were gone.

INDEX

(Page numbers in *italic* are those on which illustrations appear.)

ABOUT THE AUTHOR

LOUISE C. BROWN is a free-lance writer and former foreign correspondent who has contributed numerous articles to magazines, newspapers, and textbook publishers.

A graduate of Smith College and mother of six, she has devoted much of her spare time to community-sponsored education projects wherever she and her family were living. She has been a day-care center teacher, a founder of a cooperative nursery school, a kindergarten aide, a remedial reading tutor, an instructor of literacy courses, a publicity director for a student-exchange program, and a fund-raiser for a private school.

She now lives in Berkeley, California, where she has been working with several ecology organizations and writing about wildlife for children. She is the author of *Elephant Seals*.

ABOUT THE PHOTOGRAPHER

AUDREY ROSS is an artist, designer, jeweler, and inventor, as well as a photographer and photo editor. Her work has appeared in many magazines, textbooks, and travel books. In the two years she has spent in East Africa, she has driven safaris and collected artifacts for anthropological collections, while taking pictures of her favorite subjects, animals in the wild.

The mother of two grown children, she lives with her husband, writer and management consultant Allen Harrison, in Santa Fe, New Mexico.